莱特兄弟

Heroes and Role Models | Non-Fiction Series

Copyright © 2022 by Level Learning, INC. and Washington Yu Ying PCS™
Original and Edited Text Copyright © 2022 by Washington Yu Ying PCS™

All rights reserved. No part of this book in whole or part may be reproduced without written permission from the publisher.

Published by Level Learning, INC.

Content Contributors:
Washington Yu Ying PCS™
Level Learning - Jingyao Qi

Illustrations by: Josh Taira

Leveling classification based on Level Learning standard. For full description, visit www.levellearning.com

ISBN 978-1-64040-037-5
Traditional Chinese Edition

About Level Learning:

Level Learning provides a literacy focused curriculum specifically designed for K-12 Chinese as a Second Language classrooms. Our program offers 20 levels of specific and detailed objectives, leveled texts and passages, mastery-based online assessment, and analytics to enable data-driven instruction. Level Learning reading curriculum for both literature and informational text emphasize grammar and comprehension skills to help teachers develop confident and independent Chinese language readers. The non-fiction series of books are specifically designed to support our informational text course based on multiple national standards. To learn more about our entire offering, visit www.levellearning.com.

About Washington Yu Ying PCS™:

Washington Yu Ying PCS is a Mandarin English dual language immersion International Baccalaureate (IB) World school. Yu Ying's mission is to inspire and prepare young people to create a better world by challenging them to reach their full potential in a nurturing Chinese/English educational environment. Yu Ying's comprehensive IB, dual immersion curriculum equips students with global competencies for success in the real world. As a leader in immersion education, Yu Ying is determined to advance Chinese language programs and global citizenry education by helping other schools create and strengthen their Chinese programs. For more information, email: products@washingtonyuying.org

萊特兄弟出生在美國，分別出生於1867年和1871年。

他們的爸爸經常出去旅行，旅行回來後會帶一些東西給他們。

有一次，爸爸送給萊特兄弟一個玩具。這個玩具是用軟木、橡皮筋和紙做的，可以飛起來。

他們非常喜歡這個玩具。從那時開始,他們就想自己發明一個可以讓人飛起來的東西。

長大後,他們開了一家自行車店。下班後,他們就一起研製可以飛的東西。

他們看小鳥用翅膀飛行，翅膀後面的羽毛可以讓小鳥飛向不同的方向。

萊特兄弟向小鳥學習。他們一次又一次地試驗。後來，他們終於發明了第一架可以坐人的飛機。

1903年12月17日,萊特兄弟用他們自己的飛機飛行了59秒,852英尺。

萊特兄弟發明的飛機改變了人類歷史，他們是偉大的發明家。

Glossary

	Pinyin	English Definition
兄弟	xiōng dì	brothers
美國	měi guó	United States of America
分別	fēn bié	respectively
經常	jīng cháng	often, frequently
旅行	lǚ xíng	to travel
玩具	wán jù	toy
軟木	ruǎn mù	cork, a type of wood
橡皮筋	xiàng pí jīn	rubber band
紙	zhǐ	paper
發明	fā míng	to invent
自行車店	zì xíng chē diàn	bicycle shop
研製	yán zhì	to develop
翅膀	chì bǎng	wing
飛行	fēi xíng	flight, flying

	Pinyin	English Definition
羽毛	yǔ máo	feather
方向	fāng xiàng	direction
學習	xué xí	to learn
試驗	shì yàn	to experiment
飛機	fēi jī	airplane
秒	miǎo	second
英尺	yīng chǐ	foot, a measure of distance
人類	rén lèi	human race
偉大	wěi dà	great
發明家	fā míng jiā	inventor

www.ingramcontent.com/pod-product-compliance
Lightning Source LLC
Chambersburg PA
CBHW041223070526
44584CB00001B/74